The 1ne Page Manager

By
Donald M. Urbaniec
and
Robb Robbins

Published by
DMU & Associates
21W041 Monticello, Lombard, IL 60148
E-mail: urbaniec@comcast.net

Dedicated to
my lovely wife,
Maryann

Table of Contents

Whether you are the boss or one of the workers, this book was written for YOU!

In today's high pressure corporate environment, corporate executives, managers and workers have little time or patience with heavy work-loads, deadlines, policies or personality differences. The name of the game is "sink or swim"...which often applies to the boss as well as the workers.

"Bosses from hell" are giving U.S. workers the Monday blues. Gallup's 2013 State of the American Workplace reports 70% of those surveyed either hate their job or are completely disengaged.
Source: New York Daily News, June 2013

But the primary reason for the discontent may not be the work-load, as much as it poor communications and direction. The One Page Manager, is a manager's and worker's survival guide, which identifies and simplifies goals, priorities and tasks to insure that everyone is working from the same page and benefiting from their improved accomplishments.

Whether you are a decision maker or task manager; whether you are a doctor, lawyer, banker, engineer, sales person or staff employee, your ability to organize and manage your goals and expectations determines your success. Planning, managing, tracking and reporting progress in today's fast-paced business environment can be nearly impossible.

The principals behind *The One Page Manager* transcend all professions, industries and managerial levels to organize, prioritize and turn one's tasks and thoughts into manageable and achievable goals. Written by a former Director of Marketing, working for Fortune 500 manufacturing corporations, The One Page Manager is much more than a "daily thing-to-do "list. It is, in fact, a planning system designed to plan, manage and track the progress of every task necessary for your success.

If you work for a company and use *The One Page Manager* system, the following applies:
*   It can help you get a raise, promoted or both.
*   It can help you keep your job in a struggling economy.
*   It can help you get a better job in the future.

You are the manager:
*   Of your job
*   Of your career
*   Of your destiny

Introduction

The Purpose of this book

There is a saying in real estate I'm sure everyone has heard. It is a question-and-answer scenario: "What are the three most important things in real estate? The answers:"Location. Location. Location." If there is a counterpart for the three most important things in business, the answers would be "Results. , Results. , Results."

Ask any president if results are the key to success and you will get a re-sounding "Yes!" Ask that same president if he or she has a system for achieving results and you will get such answers as"ur,""um,"and"well . . ."Ironic, isn't it? "Results" may be the most important word in business, yet most presidents cannot produce evidence of a system for achieving them.

The purpose of this book is to provide business managers with a system for achieving results--period.

Defining Results

A key factor in defining a result is often synonymous with achieving and measuring results and how you measure them. The following list identifies some major criteria often used to **define and measure results**:

1. **Increased sales**
2. **Increased profits**
3. **Money saved through the reduction of costs**
4. **Increased productivity**
5. **Completed projects relating to all of the above**

Although this list can be expanded, these few criteria are extremely important in the growth of any business. Inherent in achieving results and using these criteria to measure them is the **unit** of measurement and **the recording** of these criteria. Either controlling the jobs that produce these results or actually performing the functions requires the recording of increases or decreases that identify results. Without such a system, the company would be unable to identify those achievements.

The *One Page Manager* helps the company create such a system.

Chapter 1

Who should read this book

This book is intended for use by all levels of business management, including:

1. All business professionals
2. Management (vice presidents and managers)
3. Presidents, CEOs, owners

Each level of management will have different work requirements demanding more or less effort. It may be assumed higher management levels are more supervisory, thus requiring subordinate level managers to create and submit the documents discussed later in this book. However, it's imperative that, regardless of your level, you understand the processes involved in creating and measuring the results.

All Business Professionals

If you are a salaried employee (as opposed to hourly), and one who is balancing numerous tasks and responsibilities, you are the professional who will benefit most from The One Page Manager system.

Regardless of your particular field of expertise, almost everyone in business reports to someone in a higher position. Often, those to whom you report have little or no sympathy for the demands of your particular position and can sometimes be difficult to work with.

How do you survive working with such a person? It is important to understand that many bosses are not intimate with the job you are performing. Their job consists of managing a staff and reporting to their bosses. In short, they don't really know what you do, but they definitely know the results you are supposed to produce.

What makes your position and them so difficult is reconciling your responsibilities (what you do) with their perception of your accountabilities (what they want you to do). Careful, they may not be wrong from their viewpoint, nor are you in yours. The key here is the word reconciliation, and putting the two of you together on the same one page, thus and allowing both of you to identify your most important goals.

Chapter Two shows you how to do the reconciliation and put the process to work.

Most managers or bosses do not have a method for reconciling and prioritizing goals. Most, will be impressed first, with your organization and secondly, by your initiative to make their priorities, your priorities.

I believe that, if your boss resists this method, you should find a new boss, job, or career. Anyone who does not want a subordinate to put his or her work on the line (in writing, including dates, priorities, and completion dates) should not be a manager in the first place. Now, if they "own the joint," you have a double problem. Again, get your resume ready.

Provided that you're not new to the job or the function being performed, manage yourself. This will eliminate most of the problems you face when dealing with a difficult manager.

Management: Vice Presidents and Managers

There is a need to clarify the term manager. This refers to those managers who genuinely manage people. Depending on the size of the company, this may be anywhere from the second to the fourth level position. The immediate value of The One Page Manager system for managers is that the same methodology under which they are managed, NOW applies to the subordinates they are managing. Essentially, this system can be used at any level, or tier, of management.

An old proverb, "God is in the idea, and the devil is in the details." applies here. Therefore, at all levels, project lists become an integral part of any multitasking function. As explained in Chapter Three, you must think through projects comprehensively before you do the work.

Presidents, CEOs, Owners

The primary responsibility of the president or owner is to set the direction of the company. That direction manifests itself into a "vision" that must be understood at a minimum by the key managers of the company and potentially by all who work for the company. This direction or "vision" should also be captured in the mission statement of the company. Unfortunately, this rarely happens since mission statements typically become muddled with wishes instead of reflecting reality or charting the company's direction.

Presidents crave a simple method of managing their people, which hopefully can (or could be) translated throughout company in more or less the same format. However, it is difficult to manage entirely different types of functions (finance, manufacturing, engineering, human relations, marketing and sales, and so forth) all with the same format. The *One Page Manager* accomplishes both of these requirements.

Chapter 1

The benefit of *The One Page Manager* system is that it places the responsibility of performance on the individuals performing the work, not the manager. It also creates an opportunity for individuals to expresses his or her
goals and priorities to the manager, which necessitates a dialogue about
goals between the boss and the subordinate.

Ask most presidents what they want and the answer is almost always,
"results." Ask them a further question about the difficulties involved in
getting results and their answer is usually related to the measurement of
results. Again, *The One Page Manager* system helps measure results, as
indicated by the percentage of completion of each goal.

Chapters Two, Three, and Five will explain these concepts in detail.

Efficiency Versus Effectiveness

Understanding the difference between these two concepts is very important to the success of any company. There is a common business saying
that differentiates efficiency and effectiveness: "Efficiency is doing things
right, but effectiveness is doing the right things." I believe, effectiveness is
not ONLY doing the right things but choosing the right priorities.

MAJOR POINT
It is far better to walk in the right direction than it is to run in the
wrong one.

Critical to being effective is the ability to choose right goals, since choosing
wrong ones will only produce poor or no results. How do you know when
you have chosen right goals? Tough call. I can only say intuition, experience, and help from your boss or peer group can all play an important role
in the selecting goals.

This book helps channel your effort with great emphasis on the care in goal
selection or, in other words, effectiveness. To really be effective is to tie all
this into strategic growth planning and to make sure that all the key managers and the president are heading in the same direction. Once the direction is set, this system is a great insurance policy for remaining on course.

Three Types of Goals

Before listing and explaining each type of goal, let's first look at the word
goal.

MAJOR POINT
A goal is a desired result.   It is not an objective or a strategy.

Therefore, increasing sales is a goal.   The rate of increase, the time frame, and all the measurement devices is discussed in Chapter Two, where goals transition into objectives.

Type One: Corporate or Company Goals

A company goal is determined by the highest ruling bodies within a company.   This could be the owner(s), chairman, president, CEO, or a committee given the authority to set goals. Typically, the largest and most significant goals require large-scale corporate investments of capital, time, and manpower as well as concentrated effort. Therefore, it ain't cheap! And, trying to manage too many significant goals at the same time can be dangerous (just ask the Third Reich).

Select few company goals, concentrate corporate resources and efforts, and stay on the few chosen. If you are one of the "lucky" managers who inherits a company goal, do not ignore its importance.

Type Two: Functional or Departmental Goals

A close second to corporate or company goals are departmental goals. This includes any type of goal relating to a specific department or to a function. Such departments could include finance, engineering, manufacturing, operations, sales, marketing, and human relations.   The closer a departmental goal matches a company goal determines its importance and priority ranking.   Any of the five results listed earlier would also rank high for importance or priority.

Finally, never ignore the wishes of the top echelon of a company.   If the president wants something or has been asking for something for a while, make it a goal and put it high on your list.   Ignoring these types of goals has caused many a good manager to be demoted or even lose his or her job.

Type Three: Personal Goals

Personal goals can also be important to an individual' s personal growth. Examples of such goals may include computer training, taking a course in a specific area, or calling in a consultant to improve performance.   While these goals may be important to an individual they should never be placed higher than either a company or a departmental goal.

Chapter 1

Self-Management: Controlling Your Destiny

What is self-management and how does it interact with *The One Page Manager* system?

MAJOR POINT

Self-management is a system of identifying and prioritizing your goals, submitting them to your boss, asking for your boss's input (reconciling your goals), and doing this without being asked (pro-activity).

A system for self-management is the driving force behind *The One Page Manager* and contains all the components necessary to complete the any job being performed. Self-management is the impetus behind the process.

The One Page Manager system essentially helps YOU manage your job. by utilizing the tools and allowing YOU to produce results as determined by YOUR priorities and as reconciled with whomever you work with and report to, be it your boss, a board, a partner, or client.

The responsibility, of performance is not only shared by these individuals, but is welcomed as they control their own destiny by providing input without having to ask for up-dates or inject (force) their opinions. This creates "pro-activity" so often welcomed but rarely seen.

Managing the Self-Managed

On the managerial side, managers can easily request the use of this the methodology, which vastly simplifies the reporting format (one page), considerations for multitasking activities, and variables from one department to another.

Regarding this last point, frequently key managers have multiple departments reporting to them. Managing these different functions with a common format such as *The One Page Manager* system, provides a simple format with allowances for slight modifications where necessary.

Multitasking

Businesses today, continue to require more and more from fewer people. Few companies are exempt from downsizing, which creates a greater the probability that people's functions will require more multitasking. The need for setting goals, priorities for those goals, and a project list to accomplish those goals becomes paramount, even critical. Not only are professionals required to do more in pure volume, but they are now required to perform different job activities. How? Again, goals, priorities, lists, and a heck of a lot of effort. The new world!

Why Do People Get Fired, Laid Off, Or Downsized?

You could write a book (and many people have) about this broad subject. The broadest generalization is that these workers don't produce the results desired by their supervisors. Key word: results.

MAJOR POINT
Many people get fired, laid off, or downsized because they are out of "step" with their boss or bosses.

While I don't have empirical evidence to support this statement, after thirty years of working in business, I have seen it time after time. Ironically, most of the people who are let go do not recognize that being out of "step" with their boss is the central issue of their demise. Being proactive and going to your boss to determine if he or she agrees with your goals is not important, it's critical.

You cannot do your job with your own agenda and hope to survive. Reconciling your efforts through a dialogue with your boss may not guarantee job safety, but it definitely increases the probability of it.

The One Page

The primary purpose of *The One Page Manager* is to allow YOU to better manage your job and pro-actively manage your manager, by aligning your priorities and goals to match theirs with YOU possessing the ability to accurately report the status of each goal, at any time.

If you are the President of a company you may think back to past and personal experiences, which relate to the examples and words choices described in this book. Much of what is stated here is from an employee's viewpoint rather than from the company's perspective, and since many Presidents worked their way to the top, you may have overcome similar difficulties. This is deliberate, since the discussion is from the real world and is seen through the eyes of the workers, not necessarily from the slant of management or the owners. The rest of the chapter will focus on the development, use and benefits of the One Page.

What Is the One Page?

The "one page" is the lead document, which can also be thought of as the "goals page" consisting of ALL goals for which you are responsible, in your job, including several additional and critical bits of information, all on one page. It is a one-page summary of all your tasks and responsibilities.

This may include: major events, activities, reports, projects and tasks Such a summary is necessary because, generally speaking, bosses don't help you do your job as much as they oversee your work and concentrate on criticisms, with a dash of compliment (notice there was no s after the last word).

This is not the "how" or the "who" will do the actual work, just the "what" it is you are responsible for completing.

This document will become your primary communications document for establishing priorities, managing schedules, managing your work-flow, communicating with whomever you work (including your mangers, clients, fellow workers or those whom you manage) , maintaining schedules and tracking your results. The real world is moving faster than ever before. Often, bosses are not trained to manage your work as much as they are trained to manage you. Managing people and doing the work are two different worlds.

Chapter 2

Is the Goals Page a Planning Devise?

Yes, but "what is planning?" One definition of "planning" is anticipating and preparing for future events. Most people talk planning but don't actually do it. Why? One of my pet theories is that planning, if done well, holds people accountable for their actions, and sometimes, their lack of actions. People shirk from accountability. They want the "show and tell" after they have accomplished something rather than predict outcomes beforehand.

MAJOR POINT
Are you brave enough to predict your efforts and hold yourself accountable?

Well, are you? It takes courage to step up to the plate and predict your next hit. Just remember that your boss, who is standing to your rear (no pun intended), will help you if you are shy about predictions.

MAJOR POINT
It is not courage that is required when predicting your performance, but necessity!

Self-management using *The One Page Manager* system helps you control your own destiny. You are controlling your boss when you walk in with your goals page and demonstrate where you are with every item on the list and compare it against theirs, which is mostly verbal. Your manager will probably have a short list of anything that went wrong, but I will just about guarantee that they will not have a list of what you did right. Sure, every employee, project manager, or business owner will experience difficulties, and short-comings are sure to come up, but *The One Page Manager* "goals page" addresses both the good and the bad.

Remember the books in college which stated, "You learn by making mistakes?" While it is true...we do learn by making mistakes, in REALITY there is little forgiveness for mistakes in business. You make a mistake...You OWN IT. We live in a "Utopian" society today, in which, YOU are responsible for any error, any mistake and every missed deadline. .

If It sounds like I'm being cynical, Yup, I am. With over thirty-five years of professional work experience, I can't remember one manager who did anything EXCEPT evaluate my work. Most people in their first ten years do not need help from managers in doing their jobs, just doing their jobs better. But, you can't blame them but, *The One Page Manager* system will help you do your job better.

What about the Boss?

Let me directly address the top tier of management. You may be a business owner, the CEO, President, Vice President or a Manager of a business? Whatever your position, the higher up you are the greater your responsibility and work load, which allows little time or patience for "training" others how to work or what is expected. Thus, new hires (and even new CEOs) are given little time in which to "sink or swim". The point being, that teaching a subordinate generally adds extra time to your job; it even is expected. Most companies have an unwritten philosophy of "sink or swim." In short, the an employee is put at a desk, inside a cubical, set in front of a computer terminal and is expected to start work immediately. A short orientation takes the place of training, and the new employee is off and running . . . to sink or swim. A copy of an out-of-date job description (which human resources is hounding the supervisor to update) is given with the one-time free lunch, and that's it.

MAJOR POINT
Most bosses are too busy to help others learn their jobs.

MAJOR POINT
Most high level managers do not know and may not want to know the details of your job.

What's a Boss to Do?

Let's assume you own your own business, are a CEO or other high level Manager with a new employee or perhaps a new supplier who at least is "treading water" but not yet "walking on water" when it comes to meeting your goals or time-tables. What is the quickest, simplest way to help them synchronize their efforts to meet your goals? The simple answer is The One Page Manager system.

It is simple when you think about it, you and your employees or suppliers can agree on what is to be done, by working from the same page. The how is the responsibility of the worker, to do the work correctly, on time, and with the desired quality. Now, you're each working from the same document, the same page, which simplifies status meetings, during which priorities and dates can easily be modified to reflect new information and/or changes.

Chapter 2

Oh, incidentally, will this method works best when both for the boss and the employee use the same system. It will works all the way up to the top. The higher you go in an organization, the more this statement applies: "the greater the probability that your boss does not know the details of your job." Now, what about you? Are you ready to plan your work and work schedule?

The Goals Page

As stated earlier, the Goals Page is the lead document, which can also be thought of as the "goals page" consisting of ALL goals for which you are responsible, in your job, including several additional and critical bits of information, all on one page.

MAJOR POINT
A goal is a desired result. It is an end point that you wish to achieve.

Therefore, the Goals Page is an overview of your accumulated responsibilities, tasks and goals. Depending upon their specific interest, some managers will want to restrict your goals to those of their particular interest however, you will undoubtedly have more. Remember, most people don't understand the details of your job, even though you must attend to each detail regardless. Conclusion: list both "your" goals and the ones you share in common with your boss, your client, partner or committee.

1. The Format of the Goals Page

This is not the "how" or the "who" will do the actual work, just the **"what"**. This may include: major events, activities, reports, projects and tasks.

 I would recommend that you do a first-cut list of goals on a separate piece of paper. Labor over this task--it is important!

Each listed goal should adhere to these characteristics:
1. It is only one line in length.
2. It description defines the result that you are seeking in terms of a completion.
3. It is concise, not verbose.
4. It does not contain **how** you will accomplish your listed goal.
5. It is the **what** of the subject matter.

MAJOR POINT
A goal is what you need to do, not how to do it.

In short, you need to list (a word you will hear a lot about) all the projects, items, and major tasks you need to complete. Don't include how, but only what. The real necessity is to state the goal in as few words as possible and hopefully on one line Stating your goal concisely is very important.

Synonymous with the importance of establishing the **right goals,** is identifying the truly important goals. Examples might include goals such as, attaining specific sales targets, reducing costs, increasing production levels, or achieving a personal achievement. The point being, these goals may be VERY IMPORTANT, whether or not their achievement is specifically included in your daily or weekly list of tasks to complete. Special attention must also be given to any duty that you have messed up or other issues that have been identified. Then you need to list these as items as goals.

MAJOR POINT

When in doubt, list the goal. Remove it after your first review with your boss if the goal is not deemed important.

I cannot stress the importance of this first list. As stated earlier, choosing right goals is vastly more important than implementing the wrong ones!

If you cannot differentiate between the important and the unimportant in your job, or if you are having real problems determining this point find a new job where you can. Or, seek immediate help from your boss for guidance, but with a trial list in your hand. The exceptions to this situation are when you are relatively new to the job, when there is no job description, or when your boss just has not had the time to train you. If you have been on the job for several months and the boss has not found the time to train you, either go above your boss for help or seek new employment.

MAJOR POINT

If your goals are wrong, all else that follows will be too!

Next, we need to add some time parameters.

Chapter 2

2. The Time Parameters

Date Started:	Due Date:	Date Completed:
_____	_____	_____

I'm sure if you've read materials or taken a course on time management or multitasking? And, no doubt you've been exposed to some type of time parameter, which you can attach to your chosen goals. I believe there are three critical time parameters which must be attached to every goal. They are:

1. The start of the item **(date assigned)**
2. The date the item is due **(due date)**
3. The date the item is really completed **(date completed)**

The three time parameters become three columns. The first column is the **date assigned**, the second column is the **due date,** and the third is the actual **date completed**.

Probably the most important is the **due date**.

MAJOR POINT
Whenever a project, report, or major activity is assigned to you, establish a firm date when the assignment is due.

Obviously, a **Due Date** is import
ant. The due date is actually more than important. For many goals due dates are critical. Due Dates are often determined by other events, functions, market or department goals with fixed time-lines. Be sure to get or set a due date for EVERY GOAL In the event you report to client, or a manager in a higher position within your company, get a due date from them.

Now comes the tricky part. If you don't **establish the due date**, you have just walked into a "trap". From time to time a task or goal has been delegated to your boss, who then delegates it to you. If your boss asks the status of the item or goal and is not pleased with your answer--the "well, er, um" syndrome--you're the likely lamb to be offered to the gods. Only your boss is deciding the goal's urgency.

OK, the due date is assigned, but your plate is full. You look at the due date and realize that you have, in your opinion, too much to do and not enough time to do it. You should try to negotiate a more reasonable time and the Goals Page can help. Using it as a visual means to make your case, or at least to adjust other priorities or get extended time for other goals. Without the Goals Page you are handicapped because the item under discussion is isolated. The list of goals supports your case.

The important aspect of *The One Page Manager* system is that YOU remain organized, in control and aware of every aspect of your goals and assignments. Nothing of significance is left to "memory". One does not need to lie awake at night worrying about the status of each task or goal, wondering if you forgot something. But the greatest aspect of The One Page Manager, is the system of communications you have (and to some extent, the shared responsibility) for prioritizing and achieving your goals with your managers.

The One Page Manager system, is also perfect for business owners and project manager working with large clients or when addressing committees overseeing large projects.

Date Assigned and Date Completed

The two dates that need further explanation are the **date assigned** and **date completed.** It is important to record the date assigned for two reasons. This date is important as it marks the date when work first began or could have begun to achieve this goal. As time and work progresses to completion you are better able to assess how much time is needed to complete similar tasks. As you become proficient in completing projects and assignments on time, the Goals Page provides evidence of your competency as well as ammunition for future raises and promotions or more projects from your clients. You become a doer, documenter, and a person who gets things done (the business management word is closure).

If you are honestly trying to play your job straight--with real dates (no hedging the dates for your benefit)--you are documenting your performance. Trust me. Very few people ever consider using a system that documents their performance to the key decision makers unobtrusively, yet publicly. (Spiking the ball in football may be acceptable, but you'll be penalized for sure if you do it in your business environment.) If your company insists you follow a separate system, use both systems, if at all possible. Your system can work in parallel to any system your company employs.

Finally, filling in the date completed column should be a labor of love, especially if it is a meaningful project or goal.

Chapter 2

The date completed, can be a testament to your efficiency and success, or identify areas where improved systems, supplier performance or adjusted time-lines need to be addressed. If you assigned your own due date and you are late, evaluate your ability to predict results involving a time parameter. Remember, one of Murphy's Laws states that everything takes longer than you anticipate. On the other hand, chronic lateness may mean that you do not set realistic time parameters when you plan. However, don't not (I know it is a double negative) set due dates that you believe in, since due dates are the best indicator of higher management potential. In short, go for it and get better over time, but keep an eye out for your completion dates and the results you are achieving.

The more often you can complete goals and record the successes before the assigned due date, the louder the "Date Completed" column speaks for YOU.

3. Setting Priorities

Two more columns are ESSENTIAL to the goals page. They are: **Your Priority** and **Your Bosses Priority**.

Priorities
Your Boss   You

_____   _____

With the multitude of responsibilities in business today, handling the most urgent tasks first, is essential. But, priorities cannot always be established simply by the earliest Due Date of each goal. You may have an event that is a very high priority but is months away. It still looms as one of the important flags to be raised when a priority is assigned. But here-in lies the real significance of The One Page Manager: First, YOU are already organized and know all the goals you need to achieve. You are not relying on your "memory", hoping you haven't forgotten anything or any important dates. You know what you've got on your plate and the status of every goal. And Second, *The One Page Manager's* "goals page" gives you a platform to discuss every goal, time-table, due date, and PRIORITY with your boss!

If you have the Date Started and the Due Date locked in you can move to the next step--setting priorities.

All too often, *NEW* goals and assignments interrupt the attention and progress of other goals. When this happens, it is time for you to re-prioritize your goals. There are really two sets of priorities: yours and your boss's. The two priorities become two columns, much like the time parameters just discussed. Why two columns? Simple. Few managers want to prioritize your goals for you. Most would prefer you to state your priority and have you go on record as to what you feel is important to the success of your job. After you have stated your position, most bosses or clients will be happy to tell you their priorities. YOU have the opportunity to be pro-active and update your manager on the progress of every goal on which you are working. It give you the opportunity to address issues interfering with progress, but most importantly it gives **you and your Boss the opportunity to identify and agree on priorities together.**

Setting Your Priorities and Ranking Them

While every job is different and the goals per the job will vary, most jobs will have from five to twenty tasks or goals on the list. For the purposes of this exercise, we will assume that there are over a dozen goals or items.

MAJOR POINT
The asterisk (*) is the start of the process of setting priorities.

What is the point of an asterisk? Well, the mind works in phases. We all seem to want to do things a step at a time, but the kicker is that the mind will "dump" (I love that word) things out in a rather random fashion. The mind will not organize something as much as it will present a group of things that are important but that are not yet organized in a sequential fashion. Here is how you work with this "mind matter":

1. You make a list of goals--your first cut.
2. You put the list away for a day, and probably you will remember ber several other potential goals or items. You add the new ones to the bottom of the existing list.
3. The new list totals twelve items or goals.
4. You look at the list and try to separate the very importan from the important. Why? Everything on the list is important, or else you would not have put it on the list in the first place, right? Now, however, you are looking for the most or very important items.

MAJOR POINT
The old 80/20 rule: Only 20 percent of what you have listed will pro mote you, enhance your image, or get you fired if you screw up.

The key is identifying the 20 percent! Let me give you real insight into your mind and its powers. Your mind will not organize, sequence, or rank everything the first time; rather, it will dump information in a random order. Therefore, you must look at the list and start with the asterisk the most important items, and separate them from the rest of the list.

5.   Put an asterisk outside of the goals or items you feel are the most important, but don't do more than five or six.

6.   Review the list and the five or six asterisked goals. Now rank the goals you have asterisked, from the most important to the least important. Put a small number one next to the most important followed by a two, and so on, until the five or six are numbered.

7.   You now have a list of the five or six most important goals you need to accomplish, along with their due dates. In short, you've just completed the most important list of goals and have ranked them in your perceived priority.

It's over, right? Nah, only the first part is. What about how your boss or client feels and what does he or she perceive to be the priority? Now the fun beginith!

Learning What Your Boss's Priorities Are for Your Job

This part is one of the major ingredients in self-managing. You don't control your manager's input, such as what he or she feels is important or their priority; rather, you control the method of the input. By first giving your manager your ideas (your list of goals), he or she perceives your genuine need for input. In short, it's their input **but your process.**

You now can take your work and create the two columns mentioned previously. Write your initials (or your first name if it is short) in the second column. Next, set up a column to the immediate left of yours and write in your boss's initials (see the example at the end of this chapter).

Now in your column, rank your asterisked (*) goals. Leave the goals in a random order, which makes it seem as though you're still determining the rankings of the listed goals. So, if you have twelve goals, six will have an asterisk with a small number from one to six found just to the right of the asterisk. The remaining goals will not have any ranking.

Take your boss's column and add lines, which allows him or her to set up their ranking system. This space will allow your boss to mark the goals he or she feels are important.

MAJOR POINT
Managers will mostly select just a few of your goals as important. This is the 80/20 rule in action.

It's rare that a manager will prioritize more than a few of your goals, since they are generally focused on the more important goals and not the total spectrum of your duties or responsibilities. The number of goals you both agree upon will probably only be three or four.

MAJOR POINT
Leave space after you have listed all of your goals.

Be sure to put in some blank spaces for additional items or goals. This allows your boss to bring up a goal or two during your review session that you might not have listed. This method can make you a hero by anticipating new input within your Goals Page. Managers love to bring up the "whatabouts": they will look at you and say, "what about this . . . or what about that." Therefore, incorporate this into your overview strategy.

4. % Completion

This column is where the tires hit the road. In the beginning, it is just another column, but as your production on all your goals and projects continue, this column will be a major indicator of your results. It is imperative that you maintain an honest evaluation of your progress for each item listed. Continued hedging or inaccurate reporting, on your part, in this column will result in your boss's lack of confidence in you--a potentially deadly situation.

Essentially, the percentage of completion should be a handy, best guess of where you feel the goal is, relative to its completion. Occasionally, a project will take three to four months to complete and perhaps involves other team members.   By assessing its completion, your manager gets a sense of the status of each project and of your management abilities.

5. The Comment Section

Comments:

_____

You need to consider the unforeseen. Something is going to happen to one or more of your listed goals that will make their completion nearly impossible, or will at least affect the timing. When this happens, **and it will**, you need a mechanism which allows you to alert your boss to a problem or circumstance that potentially could affect the estimated due date and completion of the goal. If this circumstance could delay the completion of any goal, you must immediately publish (make a copy of) your Goals Page and write a short comment describing the circumstance.   Then, follow up with a detailed description regarding the occurrence either by e-mail or memo. Remember to keep a copy of ALL your correspondence including ALL correspondence you receive regarding this matter. Is this covering your rear? Yup, but it is being done with solid business procedures.

This type of happening is fairly normal in every business. The key is not that it happens but how you handle it. You are not trying to make anyone look bad; rather, you're just protecting your goals and the deadlines that you have published, since you'll be held accountable for the results of the goal.

One word of caution: Don't make this into a campaign to identify or push off the blame to another co-worker or supplier. The point here is simply to identify a problem. The need to keep copies of the correspondence is simply to provide you some insurance if the occurrence turns into a "federal offense," which is business jargon for something that escalates beyond control. While this can happen, most often the problem is just a speed bump rather than a barrier requiring detours, repairs, and so forth.

Another method of adding comments is to develop a code for them, for instance, using a capital "A" for your first comment in the comment section. On a separate piece of paper, you describe under "A" the problem or explanation you feel should be brought to your boss's attention. You then can use the rest of the alphabet similarly for any other comments which are too long for the space provided.

6. The Horizontal Format

Why not produce this overview in the normal vertical (portrait view) format rather than the horizontal (landscape view) format on the computer? A one-word answer: space. You are creating a document with seven columns, one of which requires a description (the comment section). The horizontal format allows room for the seven columns with a brief description in the comment section.

7. Set Up a "template" File Marked "Goals Page"

Keep your overviews in this file and don't delete the completed ones written on your computer. Merely wipe your cursor across the columns, click save, and set up a new page with your margins preserved. Then make the *NEW"* changes with the new information, updating the old dates and times.

The Example Overview

Here is a brief summary of the contents which should remain consistent with every overview you produce. The contents are stated relative to the columns on the Goals Page, described from left to right.

1. **Priorities** is the column heading with two sub-columns: your boss's initials and your initials, or your first names if they are short.
   a. Your sub-column will include the numbered asterisks for only the ranked goals.
   b. Your boss's sub-column will have a line on which to enter his or her ranked priorities.
2. The next or third column will contain your concisely stated Goals.
3. The time parameters will have three columns, which should be stacked to conserve space on the page:
   a. Date Started
   b. Due Date
   c. % of Completion the column is small in length, with just enough room for a number and the % sign (e.g., 40%).
4. Date Completed
5. The column is the Comment column is as long as the space left on the horizontal line. A tip here is to go to the page setup in your word processing program and enlarge the horizontal page by reducing the margins to as small as possible. This will maximize the horizontal portion of the page.

The following page contains a sample layout of the Goals Page. You can create it in Microsoft Word using standard margins for your guides or any spread sheet format (e.g. Excel) and adjust the lengths of the columns accordingly. Your call. Depending upon the complexity or your responsibilities, one page could turn into two pages, but this is rare. Try to keep it to one. Another tip is to eliminate spaces between the items listed and/or use a small font size Matrixes

GOALS PAGE
(always include a new date when updating the overview)
Date: _____

Priorities Your Boss	YOU	Goals	Date Started	Due Date	% Of Completion	Date Completed	Comments
	*6	1. Develop a new database for Preferred Customer Program					
	*4	2. Coordinate the Sales Meeting to be held in Atlanta					
		3. Chair the Quality Circle task force to assess company morale					
	*5	4. Submit report on product improvements					
	*2	5. Reduce complaints in Preferred Customer Program					
	*3	6. Assist in developing a new brochure for the Preferred Customer Program					
	*1	7. Launch direct mail program to support sales					
		8. Analyze leads received from AST & Assoc.					
		9. Develop new format for phone inquires					
		10. Track hours per week assisting Personnel Dept.					
		11. Create new time pages for supplier usage					
		12.					
		13.					
		14.					
		15.					
		16.					

The Matrix

Turning company goals into results: The Matrix

Earlier, we covered the three types of goals:
- a. Company Goals
- b. Departmental Goals
- c. Personal Goals

This chapter will focus on YOU being the lucky one, who is assigned a strategic company goal, either by a committee of company managers, the president (and/or owner), or both.   To serve as an example of the how and why you use a matrix, the following is given to you.: You are the Director of Sales and Marketing for a small company whose strategic goal is determined to be, "increase NEW sales by $1,000,000, incrementally, in the next calendar year.

Let me provide some insight into what you might be facing. Remember the commercial a few years ago with a person seated at a desk and who is obviously talking to his boss.   He is saying a bunch of, "I can do that's" and agreeing to be in different cities in nearly consecutive days, after which, he hangs up the phone, looks at the camera and says, "How am I going to do that?"

You have been told to increase sales by $1,000,000 within a one year's time period representing an increase of 20% above last year's sales. This is a real killer goal by any stretch of effort. You look in the mirror and say, "How am I going to do that?"   The real answer is the same way you eat an elephant. One bite at a time! But, where do you start?

Begin with the MATRIX.
(Not the movie, but the one page.)

The business definition of a matrix is as follows and it has four components:
- A.   A goal which is a generalization of what you or your company wants to accomplish.
- B.   An objective that defines the goal in specific terms.
- C.   Multiple strategies explaining how you will plan to accomplish the goal.
- D.   Finally, the tactics identifying the detailed tasks required to accomplish each strategy chosen.

Each of these ingredients will be explained in the following pages.

Chapter 3

MAJOR POINT
- Don't look at the KISS acronym: Keep It Simple Stupid
- Use the "One Page Manager" version, MISS: Make It Simple Stupid

The ultimate point here is that making a million dollars for a company requires a methodology that is both simple in format, yet covers complicated or involved solutions. While comprehensive, each task becomes a simple means of communications. The matrix will provide such a vehicle.

Before turning to the matrix itself, we need to explain several critical concepts which the matrix will evolve into. One other major point needs to be made about using the matrix concept and the frequency of its use.

MAJOR POINT
The use of the matrix should be restricted to major company goals as it is too involved to be a one-line item on the ordinary Goals Page and might adulterate those important goals with frequency of use.

Let us look at the elements necessary to produce an effective matrix.

1. Goal

A goal is a generalization of what you or your company wants to do (the desired result).

In this example, the **Goal is to Increase sales by $1,000,000**.

What is an objective versus a goal?

2. Objectives

An objective is what you do, which then leads to increased results. The objective must also meet three important criteria:
- **A.** **It must be measurable.**
- **B.** **It must be over a defined time parameter.**
- **C.** **It must be realistic.**

The key word is "**what.**" It's key because if you don't select your "whats" carefully, you've started down the wrong path regardless of **how** you do anything.

MAJOR POINT
What you do is infinitely more important than **how** you do it.

There have been countless meetings where words like "**objective**" or "**purpose**" were used with care for a few seconds, maybe even a few minutes. The rest of the meeting (sometimes two to three hours long) was spent strategizing **how** something could be done, only to learn much later that the **what** was wrong.

People love to spend time strategizing about **how** to do something, but refuse to spend time correctly choosing the measurable objectives in the beginning. If the criteria mentioned earlier were used to make sure the right objective/purpose was selected, and if the first half-hour was spent discussing whether or not the objective is solid to begin with, and if the objective was researched to make sure that it was something worth accomplishing, then companies would make much more money and would not waste valuable time and effort.

MAJOR POINT
An objective is the expansion of a goal that includes the three criteria.

Using a non-marketing/sales example, a goal could be to "lose weight". It would not be an objective because it does not fit the criteria listed earlier. However, the goal is the person's wish for an end result he or she would like to attain. The objective of the goal could read something like: lose one pound per week for twenty weeks, with no more than five pounds regained at the end of the twenty-fifth week. The criteria is met because the objective is quantified, over time, it addresses a reasonable weight loss per week, as well as the bounce-back that nearly always accompanies a weight-loss program. It is a sound objective to achieve a weight-loss goal.

Stating the objective

In the beginning of this section, the issue of selecting your **whats** carefully was addressed. The critical word to add is **why** if you don't feel the **what** is on target. **Why** are we going to do this? If we do, how much will we make, in what time period, and based on what premise, conclusion, or data? Spread out the questions so as not to intimidate the person or persons who might be suggesting the objective, but ask these questions. A good objective will stand the test of these questions. Look at a sample of an objective that is marketing/sales driven derived from our goal.

To add twenty new customers in the year 2014, each of which will do $20,000 in new sales and will increase to $50,000 by the end of 2015.

1. Does it lead to a **desired result?** Yes, in that the desired result is new sales. It claims it will achieve the new sales by adding customers, but it doesn't say how, because that will come from the strategies that need to be developed.
2. Is the objective measurable? Yes, twenty customers, $20,000 in 2000, $50,000 in 2014.
3. Does the objective have a time parameter? Yes, both 2014 and 2015.
4. Is the objective **realistic**? Tough call. The answer to this question lies in the research or knowledge of the writer of the objective or the departments consulted. If the person suggesting the objective researched the average customer base to determine that all customers divided by the total sales is $50,000, and if it would take two years to reach this figure ($20,000 the first year), the answer would be "yes." Second, did the person ask or research the numbers with the finance department and MIS or both? The key here is accuracy and homework/teamwork. If the person is picking the number from his or her memory, beware. The numbers have to stand up to the **whys** that should be asked.

If the objective is weak, vague, or too general, it will not hold up in the long run. This will result in poor respect for the process, causing the team of key players to speak one thing publicly (in meetings) but to doubt the planning process privately--creating a very serious company problem.

How many objectives?

The question goes back to the company strategic goals. Too many goals prompt too many objectives. Having too many objectives and too many goals can create premature optimism that leads to potential failure for parts of the growth plan. Can you afford to do everything? Do you have the resources to consider many goals and objectives?

The answers to these questions lie in the budget section. Remember, there should be a few goals resulting in a few objectives, many strategies, and many more tactics. Try to arrange each goal and objective in a flowchart to test each individually so you can determine if you have too many. Combine the flowchart with the budget section and you have the critical indicators.

Chapter 3

MAJOR POINT

A strategic goal turns into one objective (by adding the three criteria), but an objective has multiple strategies and multiple supporting tactics.

It is possible to have more than one objective supporting one goal, but this would be the exception rather than the rule. Pushing you strategic goal through this outlined process insures uniformity, simplifies the complicated, and adds clarity in accomplishing you goal, alias obtaining results.

3. Marketing Strategies

Providing you have chosen your goal and objective correctly, the next critical step is selecting your strategies. Let's return to the definition of strategy:

A strategy is **how** you're going to do something. It must be targeted to an audience, and it is a derivative of the marketing mix. In short, it is the "how" and "who" of doing something. The marketing strategy in this example encompasses two basic elements:

- **A.** **The marketing mix (how you do something):**
  1. **Product**
  2. **Price**
  3. **Place/Channels of distribution**
  4. **Promotion**
  5. **People (the sales force)**
- **B.** **The market target (who is the strategy aimed at)**

This section will contain lists of information pertaining to these areas. Selection is the critical task. While there is a great deal of science and research that can be used during the selection process, experience and "intuitive" factors play a heavy role in deciding which one or ones to use. Experienced personnel may have a strong intuitive sense about what could be wrong but may not be able to easily verbalize it. Any company is well served by flushing out these perspectives. Therefore, this section is more a checklist or a guide than it is a recipe for success.

Chapter 3

Here is a conceptual drawing of the flowchart process with an understanding that we have yet to discuss the strategies and tactics sections. It is presented here to make sure the reader looks carefully at the objectives and how they were reached.

Goal, Objective, Strategies , Tactics Flowchart

	Goal		
	Objective		
Strategy	Strategy	Strategy	Strategy
Tactic	Tactic	Tactic	Tactic
Tactic	Tactic	Tactic	Tactic
Tactic	Tactic	Tactic	Tactic

First, let's review the earlier examples given and add four selected strategies to accomplish the chosen goal and objective:

Goal (Direction)
Target new customers, resulting in $1,000,000 in new sales.

Objective
Add twenty new customers in 2014, each of which will do $20,000 in new sales (define the "What") and will increase to $50,000 by the end of 2015.

Strategies
Check off the marketing mix strategizer & target market selected ("How").

    #1   Direct Mail:
Create a direct mail campaign to the xxxxxx SIC code customers and qualify the lead obtained.

    #2   Training:
Develop a training program for field sales to obtain and increase sales to the desire level of $50,000 in two years.

    #3   Literature
Assign and coordinate a series of direct mail brochures with the marketing communications agency.

    #4   Collateral:
Develop both training and collateral materials internally to use with the field sales force.

4. Tactics (details)

A tactic is the "**details**" of the strategy, broken down by the specific actions to be performed. Many books speak of tactical marketing with the understanding that the key to success is in the details rather than the overview. You need both.

Next, let's show an example of what one chart might look like, noting that the example is simple and illustrates the logic behind the sequence of a goal, objective, strategies, and tactics. The real objective would have to include more tactics than is shown, but this simple example shows multiple strategies and tactics, side by side (see following page). Secondly, the example provided on the next page concentrated on the marketing function to illustrate the process of creating the matrix structure. In the real world, there most likely would be strategies involving other departments and other functions such as accounting, manufacturing, operations etc.

Goal
(To target new customers, resulting in $1,000,000 in new sales.)

Objective
(To add twenty new customers in 2014, each generating $20,000 in new sales and increasing to $50,000 by the end of 2015.)

Strategy #1 (Direct Mail)	Strategy #2 (Training)	Strategy #3 (Literature)	Strategy #4 (Collateral)	Strategy #5 (Advertising)
Tactics	Tactics	Tactics	Tactics	Tactics
a. Rent a list of SIC codes for 1,000 customers.	a. Schedule meetings for preliminary discussions.	a. Contact agency for preliminary meetings and cost estimates.	a. Have preliminary meeting with new agency.	a. Contact agency for objective meeting.
b. Produce 6 sets of labels per each customer name.	b. Conduct interviews with field sales personnel.	b. Get rough layout of brochures.	b. Submit outline developed by sales managers.	b. Set schedule for new advertisement and its development.
c. Design bounce-back card for reply/qualification system.	c. Outline the program and get management approval.	c. Sign off on all copy.	c. Get approval for rough materials that sales personnel will use.	c. Get quote for campaign.
d. Install 800 number.	d. Develop outline for sales plan.	d. Approve final layout and film.	d. Produce flip chart for sales presentations.	d. Get media schedule and costs for placement.
e. Set up telemarketing company for follow-up.	e. Set schedule for all regional sales plans and their completion.	e. Print all brochures.	e. Produce slide presentation for upper management.	e. Complete new ad.
f. Write lead letters for campaign.			f. Develop customer tours and new showroom.	f. Place ad in media.
				g. Qualify leads with the direct mails qualification system.

The Project Page

What is it and Why do it?

Nearly everyone has some form of organizational tools they use. Most people, use a simple version of a daily things to do list. Many use a printed daily organizer, a lap-top, I-phone or other hand-held electronic device. All electronics available today is good and well, but there is an important part missing from the process: true, honest to God, planning. As stated earlier, planning is predicting future events. Putting dates in a book and recording your "daily things to do" is only a small portion of planning. This fragment of the process needs to be expanded.

We've added the first major part to the equation, the Goals Page identifying the **what** portion of the process. Secondly, we have added the matrix, as a primary tool for the enlargement of the most significant strategic company goals, which is the complicated and involved **how**.

MAJOR POINT
• All projects of any significance (on your Goals Page) require thinking out and forethought
• Most projects deemed a high priority by both you and your boss need a project page

How many of you were influenced by Nike's, "Just do it!" That one expression, launched our modern world of not only people committed to exercise, but a world of "doers." OK, I am all for doing. Just do it **right** the first time. And, here comes the magic word: *think*. *Think* first, and do second. I did not say think until you have missed the opportunity; just, *think* and then do. That one expression is the essence of planning.

If you've ever built a garage, remodeled or built a house, or handled a project requiring major effort and dollars, you know that without planning you're going to be in big trouble, quick. At work, we have difficulties in taking the time to *think* because of the multitudes of interruptions. As a consultant, I frequently heard people saying, "I don't have time to think" due to all the meetings, phone calls, phone mail, e-mail, texts, visits by co-workers and the list goes on.

MAJOR POINT
Make time to *think*; an hour of prior thought is worth one day of work!

Chapter 4

If you can't think or plan at work, take *thinking* and *planning* home.

"Wait a minute!" "That's my time." Yup, you bet it is. But, if you squeeze a bit, you can do it at home without too much of a problem. First, most good planning takes place on the week-end, anyway. Try doing it early Sunday morning. Kids are either watching TV or sleeping (if you are married). The hours from 8:00 to 10:00 are prime, and the best times to think about the week. Finally, there are no phone or common work interruptions and one hour planning at home has got to be worth two or three hours at work.

The Elements of a Project Page

A project page is a list of things to do, but restricted to a specific subject. You generally can't put the list on just a "daily things to do" list as the tasks may take several days or even weeks to complete. The first step in planning is organizing. Organizing always precedes planning. You have to separate your thoughts into categories and try to stay focused long enough to "dump" all the thoughts, flying around your head on each project onto separate Project Pages.

MAJOR POINT
Work on several projects at the same time using multiple pads of paper or computer pages

The "dumping" process mentioned above is generally a process of thoughts that have been bottled up in your head for a while. In addition to the one major subject you are thinking about, there are generally several others. Once you solicit your brain for a "mind dump" you will activate the other subjects and you will find those wanting out too. Go with the flow. Take several sheets or pads of paper (remember, paper is cheap but, your planning time is valuable) title each page with a different subject per your goals or objectives. Start with the subject you deemed is **most important** and record the items you feel needs to be done, the tasks pertinent to completion.

Let us stop here and first list the elements found on this simple, but important sheet of paper:

1.   The name of the project.
2.   The date started on this project.
3.   The date you and your boss agreed that you would complete this project.
4.   A space for the actual completion of this project.
5.   The margin created by either the printed line on the paper or one you draw on the page.
6.   In the upper right hand corner, the date you are creating this page.

Several things to remember: Write small, don't skip spaces (tighten up your word and spaces and it will have an effect on your thinking as well), try to print not write.   On that last part; Why print rather than write?   Because, it slows you down and when you print, you're forced to *think* a little slower and clearer.

Start the process by filling out the sheet with the above information before listing items or tasks that you know need to be completed.   Use action verbs wherever possible: go, do, see, write, develop, call, etc.   Condense your writing and don't worry about sentence fragments.   If a subject requires sub-topics, outline the item with sub part (a, b, c, d, e, etc.).   Don't try to organize the thoughts or sequence them when they are coming out.   Just go with the flow.   Remember, you are probably the only person on earth who knows what you have to do to complete this project.

Important Concepts Surrounding the Project Page

There are several things to remember about creating a Project Page.

1.   The page should not be part of another subject as this will al low additional task to be added to the single page.
2.   During a session, you will have start and stop points and need to go back to the page later.
3.   The information will be in a random order until you sequence it later.
4.   The more you do the process, the better you will become.
5.   Think about being on a latter looking down on all you need to do (a visual image).

Chapter 4

Returning to the Asterisk and Its Use

Remember the words I used in Chapter Two concerning the use of the Asterisk. Here is a repeat of what I said:

"What is the point of a asterisk? Well, the mind works sort of in phases. We all seem to want to do things a step at a time, but the kicker is that the mind will "dump," things out in rather a random fashion; your mind will not organize, sequence, and rank anything the first time. The mind will not organize something as much as it will present things in a set of things that are important, but again, not yet organized in a sequential fashion."

"Therefore, it is important you understand this process. Look at the list and just start with the asterisk * method of separating the most / very important from the important (all things on the list are important)."

6.   Put an asterisk * outside of the tasks / items you feel are the most important.
7.   Review the list and asterisked * goals. Now rank the tasks you have asterisked * from the most important to the least. Put small 1 next to the most important followed by a 2, and so on until the 5 or 6 are numbered.
8.   You now have a list of the most important tasks you need to accomplish, and have ranked them in your priority and importance.

The Importance of Doing a Project Page

General, Dwight D. Eisenhower once said, "The plan is nothing, the planning is everything." What he meant was, the process of planning, which is really thinking through a project or problem so nothing is forgotten or skipped, is more important that the paper it's written on.

MAJOR POINT
After you have written the project page, you can almost throw away the paper because, the thoughts concerning the solution are organized in your head.

Again, in this age of "Just do it!" we are doing things wrong, not doing right or doing the wrong things, and going crazy with too much to do with so little time to do it. We must take the time to think through those goals and accompanying tasks that are most important to our job.

Your Monday mornings will be a lot less stressful and in the event your boss asks for details regarding any project or task, it is readily available and underscores your efficiency and abilities. Your boss probably doesn't want to know the details of the project and its development, but he or she, will be put at ease when he sees with your planning effort and preparedness.

Updating the Project Page

As a general rule, the project list should be updated more in reference to the importance of the project than to any real rule of thumb for time. However, most projects need updating every two to four weeks (occasionally, you might need a weekly update). The important point here is if you have individual sheets, you can add points or tasks as you either think of them or as the occur. The list is dynamic, not static.

The Scope of the Project Page

Remember, it will be indeed rare that you or anyone will have the ability to plan a any project, complete with all the steps in one session. Therefore, the project page is a moving target. Think of it like a flashlight. The beam will only cover a portion of the entire project at any given time. As you move through the project (moving the beam of the flashlight) you will see more and more will be revealed. In short, the project will reveals steps yet to be taken so the document you are creating is a living document and needs updating periodically. Here is what a typical project page should look like:

Chapter 4

Date: 10-1-14

Subject: Development of Web Site for "Grow or Die: Growth Strategies for Management"
Dates:

  a. Started: 8-1-14
  b. Due: 12-1-14
  c. Completed: _____

---

	1. Set up file folders for each page on the web site
*4	a. Home
*5	b. About
	c. Testimonials
	d. Free Report
	e. Order
	f. Links
	g. E-mail
*1	2. Contact web designer for appointment to discuss the layout of the web site, content, functionality
*2.	3. List and/or sketch ideas for the web designer meeting for the structure, look and links to important information
	4. Decide upon which content management system allows the greatest ease for editing and adding site content
	5. Choose an appropriate domain name
*3	6. Choose a web hosting service
	7. Set up a business account for electronic transfers related to internet sales or a shopping cart
	8. Include a direct link to amazon.com to enable ordering the book

Self-Management

Working for a Company

This chapter is intended for use by people who are employed by a company or corporation. While there are many applications that could, and do apply for a person in their own business or are entrepreneurs, the main thrust is directed toward managers and professional people in a company producing a product or service.

This chapter will focus on the professional employee who is working for a company and desires improvement in their relationship, both with the company and their immediate supervising boss. The major criteria defining a professional is, "an educated person, salaried (not hourly) and normally working well beyond 40 or more hours per week".

The designation of "Self-Management" might then be slightly misleading. How can a person work for a company and truly be "self-managed?" Well, only when your boss fully trusts your judgment, is aware of your intentions and is confident those intentions are for the good of the company. If your boss feels that you're not a team player and are only out for your personal advancement, most likely, your boss will resist your efforts regardless of your personal successes.

A Company is People

Regardless of the size of your company, you probably interface with only a small group of people. Unless you work with a large group, which is more the exception than the rule, this small group is really "the company" for all practical purposes. Your career and its success will be determined by how well you interface with this group. If you leave the company, your attitude toward that company will be determined by your experience with the group, a part of which, will be determined by the personal or professional relationship between you and your boss.

Controlling Your Boss

Do visions of chains and ropes enter your mind when you think of your boss? Do you see yourself standing before your boss with he or she in chains and you (with a whip and a large grin) giving the orders with your boss having to listen and obeying?

Chapter 5

No. Controlling you boss is not intended to include either mind control or control by contrivance. Rather is a desired result which both parties need and want. You keep your boss informed about what you intend to do and your boss adds input, not dominating your every action which is resented by you. Controlling your boss starts with the Goals Page. But, there is much more surrounding the One Page you must also consider. This chapter gives you some sound advice and tips to keep you on your course of being self-managed.

Before going into some of the advice and tips, let's look at a few basic characteristics all companies use when evaluating personnel.

Being Successful in a Company

Attitude

In my past professional life, a former Vice-President of Sales and Marketing once called me into his office and said, "If you don't change your attitude, I'll get rid of you."

I was shocked! Me? This had never before happened in my professional life! I'd been working like a mule for over a month on several projects with "the whole banana": long hours, extreme pressure, too many balls in the air, etc. A few days earlier, a project manager who worked for the company stopped in the hall one day and said, "You don't smile anymore." I shot back over my shoulder, "Look. You give me half the work, and I will give you twice the smiles." I gloated over my quip, until I had my conversation with the Vice-President. You see, I thought that my work would speak FOR me and I wasn't worried about my attitude. **Wrong!**

That night, after his talk with me, I really did some soul searching. I hated his comment, but I knew all the factors that were bearing down on me did not excuse the grumpy and unpleasant man I had become. The next day, I walked into the Vice-President's office and apologized. Ever since that day, I've tried to maintain a positive attitude, mainly because you can't punish others through your lack of smiles and unpleasantness due to your pressures or being overworked. As the Vice-President said, "Your attitude is contagious. It spreads throughout your staff and the All the people you work with."

MAJOR POINT
Don't blame others through you attitude for your problems or pressures.

Hard work and a poor attitude still equals a potential pink slip. Just as in math, a positive and a negative still equals a negative result. Smile even when it is killing you inside.

Quick Checklist for Success

Here's a quick checklist you should review to see if you're in the right job and experiencing a lack of smiles (a big indicator of attitude and happiness) similar to my story:

1.   Are you in the right industry?
2.   Are you in the right company in that industry?
3.   Are you in the right job in the right company in that industry?

If you don't start with the right industry first, the rest might be irrelevant. Any stock brokerage firm can give you tons of information about the growth of your company's industry. The pressure of working in a dying industry potentially transfers those pressures to you. Don't work for a dying industry or one which the brokerage firm rates as "flat".

Next, what does the brokerage firm say about your company? If your company is not publicly traded, you can still research your industry sector to find out how your company stacks up to its competitors. Conversations with your sales people will give you most of what you need to know.

Finally, are you in a holding pattern relative to the job you are performing? Starting out in a new career, you might have to struggle to get to the next level, so don't pick something that's a dead-end with a poor history of moving people up. In particular, watch out for the "I got through college with the easiest degree and now I can't get something that pays well or has advancement." Go back for additional training and education to avoid locking yourself into a go-no-where scenario.

Here are two vital questions about your professional future:
1.   Are you happy doing what you are doing?
2.   Are you good at what you are doing?

If the answer to either of these questions is, NO, change something now! Regarding the second question, "Are you good at what you are doing?" If, you're a salesperson and you are doing lousy at it, stop kidding yourself, change! If you're in telemarketing, and you are not meeting your quotas, change!

Chapter 5

Getting Promoted

Whole books are written on this subject. This section will be brief, but invaluable if YOU take heed. The subjects covered will probably be unique to this book.

1. Publish Your Planning or Perish

A proverb ventured: "He who predicts accomplishments within a published (printed on paper) time period with the desired management results, will be promoted or rewarded in their company." The Goals Page is exactly the type of published material that gets you noticed and promoted.

If you're the only one in your department using The One Page Manager system and you accomplish what you predict, you will stand out. You will be noticed, and you will increase the probability of being promoted.

2. Using a System that Accomplishes Multi-Tasking

Very few professional people have just one dimension to their work. Multi-tasking is today's work world reality, but there are few books, which tell you specifically **how to do it**. Believe me, I couldn't find much help when I was handling a ton of different tasks (projects, meetings, reports, etc.) so, I created the system to make it manageable.

The next section called, "Tools" will go into all the tools I've used in my 30 years of multi-tasking.

MAJOR POINT
The more you have to do, the more the work is diversified, the more the need for different tools used as the work increases.

To summarize, the more multi-tasking required in your job, the more you need the proper tools to help you accomplish your total work load.

The Tool Box

Most of us try to accomplish our jobs with a Swiss Army Knife philosophy. What I mean is, we try to force one tool to manage everything we do. In the case of a mechanic, you'll see in the repair bay a stacked tool case... typically, red and as high as six foot. Each drawer has tools divided by type and size. A mechanic can't use just one adjustable wrench to work on your car. Likewise, you must consider different tools.

The most ineffective group of tools being used by professionals today is I-pad (or its clone), the I-phone (or its clone) and the daily planner, especially the smaller version.

MAJOR POINT
The more you have to do or wish to accomplish, the more you should use a full (8 ½ x 11) pad.

Modern technology may give the appearance of efficiency, but it's no match for pen and paper, when it comes to planning, recording or viewing complex tasks and projects.

The Goals Page

Just as you need a flight plan filed before taking off in an airplane or a system of navigation for sailing long distances, you also need a Goals Page outlining the direction of your job.

MAJOR POINT
What should always proceed **how**.

Since a whole chapter has covered this subject, there is much to say at this point, except the above Major Point is critical. And as stated earlier, if your **what** is wrong, all else will be as well. If you are doing work without the agreement of your boss, much to all of it might be in vain. Make sure your **what** is correct before you proceed on your journeys.

The Matrix

In Chapter Three, there is an involved explanation of when and why to use the matrix concept. This will be just a short review of the criteria concerning its use. In Chapter Three, I stated that you need to **make things simple** rather than keep things simple. The essence of that statement is that working in business is not a simple proposition, nor are the challenges that face professional people working in business.

When you're assigned a strategic company goal, it is always complicated and will require complicated tools to accomplish the results desired. A strategic company goal is very much like working on a modern automobile. It ain't easy. Therefore, the matrix for the goal defined will require the process suggested in the chapter. Namely, you start with the goal or result defined, move to making the goal into an objective by adding the criteria of measurement, a time parameter, and making sure it is achievable (realistic). I will about guarantee that it will require multiple strategies, and each strategy will have multiple tactics or tasks to done.   Remember that there is one goal, turned into one objective, but multiple strategies that will require multiple tactics per strategy.

MAJOR POINT
Complicated goals require complicated solutions, but made simple through the use of a matrix and presented in one page for managerial review.

Once the matrix is complete and management signs off on its logic and strategies, the most important part the "planning" is done which can be its absolute value.

Project Lists

When should you do a project list?   OK, start laughing now.   When you have a major project, "Grasshopper". Always?   Yup.   Remember, the principle reason for doing a "project list", is that it facilitates thinking.   Merely starting a project list, makes you start thinking through the project before you start.   Also keep in mind that a large project may require many steps and multiple project lists in a sequential order.   Chances are you'll not be able to think completely through an entire project until you work through the initial steps of the process. As you do, you'll see the project more clearly and additional steps will be easier to plan.

The ultimate value of a project list is that it helps you think through the project.

Weekly Overviews

Few of us can think and plan the multitude of tasks required for every project "in-process", as well as all the meeting requirements beyond a week's span.   I'm not talking about maintaining a calendar of events, which generally indicates meeting requirements.   I'm talking about each task you need to complete this week and listing each task on paper.   OK, you may be asking yourself, "Why do I need a weekly overview, if I've done my project lists?"   Simple, because your project lists typically span several weeks of tasks and these project lists are all different.   They're generally, independent lists and, therefore, specific parts of each list you wish to accomplish this week, need to be combined for this week. Remember, if you're multi-tasking, you're handling a great many different things over the course of the week. The **Weekly Overview** combines all this week's tasks into one checklist document providing a clear direction for everything you wish to accomplish this week.

Wait a minute!   You mean I have to do weekly overviews and project lists, along with maintaining my Goals Page.?   The real answer is, it depends. The more complicated your job and the projects you need to complete, the more tools you'll to keep you on track. If your work load is simple, use simple tools to accomplish it.   If your job is complicated, and many are, the more you need multiple tools.   Like the mechanic, he most likely would not use many tools to change your oil, but what about working on your transmission?   The job dictates the complexity and the tools are a function of that complexity.

The Daily Things-to-Do List

Most of us have a version of a "daily things to do list".   Few, have it down to the science I'm about to talk about. But a few are heavy hitters when it comes to producing large volumes of work and different types of work simultaneously (multi-tasking) at that.   A real tip I would like to pass on to you, is using a tape recorder in your car.   Most people are captive in a car for at least 30 minutes, one each way to and from work.   OK, you love music, talk shows, and the news when driving.   Subconsciously, you resent having to do work in your car except for the proverbial cell phone, which I claim is more a crutch than a tool.   Use the 30 minutes or so of travel time to plan your daily things to do.   Dictate your tasks as you're driving and let the time be spent planning, instead of "vegging" out.   I'll guarantee that you'll increase you productivity.

Here are some tips about using a daily things to do list.   Whenever possible, do your list either before you leave for work or at home before the next day.   I'll guarantee (again) you'll increase your productivity if you walk into work with your list prepared, versus doing it when you first arrive. Why?   The phone calls, voice mail, e-mails, mail, faxes and more ALL have a tendency to destroy your day and its direction.   If you let these things control your day, you will be far less productive.   Add **all the new input** from these areas, but don't let these areas destroy your direction.   There'll be days when the messages will rule your day or major meetings will demand you attendance, but let these be the exception, rather than the rule.

When I complete my things to do list, I then go over it and use the asterisk method for assigning my priorities for the day.   Your list is only half complete if you don't prioritize your day and the list.   Once I've listed my first six to eight items and prioritized them, my initial work load for the start of the day is done.   Now it is time to implement.   In short, to work.

Very important:
List your tasks on the full 8 ½ x 11 page. Next, single space every item you're listing. (Double spacing gives you a false sense of accomplishment, while single spacing reduces the items and illustrates what you are really doing.)

At this point, you may be asking yourself, "Is this guy for real?" "Does he really do all this stuff?" *Yup, and more.* In thirty years of working, no one ever really out-organized or out-planned me. I trained myself and developed these tools **out of necessity**. In my position in marketing and communications, with the volume of work and complexity of tasks required, it was either use these tools or go crazy. Again, the job dictates the tools needed.

The Monthly Planner

I save the monthly planner almost exclusively for meetings and important dates to remember. I don't use it for listing tasks to be performed unless it's very date sensitive. I don't wish to imply it's not an important part of the tool box, as it is.

But, it should not be used to plan as much as record and flag important events. When it's part of your planning, you should always use your project lists or matrix first, and the listing of the activity on the monthly planner, second. (The exceptions are meetings.)

The *General* Things-To-Do List

Where do you put items or tasks that you have to do, but really have a low priority for today and maybe the week? I create a sheet (yes, it is one page).

I call my General Things-To-Do list. I include personal things, in addition to my business things. Here are some examples: Buy a ream of paper for my computer at home. File the stack that's on my cadenza. Clean my office. Get my car washed. Call a friend. Talk to my boss about my vacation etc. I don't take this list lightly as is sometimes records important things, just not urgent things for today. Again, I use the asterisk method for indicating the task's relative importance.

The Tricks or Tips

1. **Use a spiral binder for taking notes in meetings:**
    Many people will use either their day planner or a note pad for taking notes in meetings. I've found that I have a propensity to lose those notes or misfile them. By having a spiral binder dedicated to only taking notes in meetings, I have a complete record of the meeting, and know where the notes of the meeting are. If I need to transfer the notes to a file, I copy the notes on a copy machine and put the copy in the file. Many, many, times this method of using the spiral binder has saved my, *well you know what*.

2. **Always leave a left hand margin on your planning pages.**
    This is a very important concept to remember. If you leave a margin in your project lists or daily things to do lists, you automatically give yourself a column for making asterisks and then ranking these in a determined order. As stated earlier, after I make my list, I add my most important asterisks, and then rank those asterisks in order of importance. My initial thinking for the day is done. I don't wish to imply that all the thinking for the day is done (as in the case of a daily things to do list), but I'm ready to engage in doing, and that first asterisk is like starting your engine. You're ready to do!

3. **The computer versus the pen & pad:**
    I can't think on a computer. I spend much of my day in front of one and can create data bases; mail merges; spread sheets; graphics and their manipulations; Power Point; websites; e-mail; and of course word processing. But, I still cannot think on a computer.

Maybe it's the author in me. But, I was in business years before my first writings and I believe, the power of the pen & pad is mightier than the computer. Thinking on paper slows you down and allows one the time to stop and think. Once you have an outline of where you are going, the computer can be an invaluable tool. I suggest using each, but separate each for the power that each possesses.

MAJOR POINT
The power of the pen and pad is mightier that the computer.

Chapter 5

4. **Printing versus writing:**
   OK, here's probably one of my greatest idiosyncrasies. I firmly believe that if you print your things to do lists, project lists, and draft of you Goals Page, you'll have a clearer thought process than if you write in script. My theory is you're slow ing down the brain. By printing, you slow down the processing of information to such a rate that thinking becomes clearer. Secondly, the process of printing shows you're thinking more clearly, as many of us have poor penmanship when writing in script. Before you laugh at this concept, try it for a week and compare your script to your printing and see if it makes a difference.

5. **Lining out the complete tasks in red versus black:**
   Writing with a red pen jumps off the page and gives a more dramatic statement you your subconscious that you've accomplished the tasks at hand. You can also read what you have done more easily, as sometimes you might want to go back over your sheets to recall when you accomplished something. I use a red pen for all my asterisks and for numbering my priorities.

   The red asterisks and corresponding numbers jump off the page. Your eye focuses on the asterisks and you are off and doing. This method works.

Accountability

The Difference between Accountability and Responsibility

It's not just important, but imperative that a CEO sit down and write a brief description of what results he needs from EVERY one of his key managers. It is not ONLY important that a manger sits down and writes a description of what results are needed for EVERY one of his people, IT'S IMPERATIVE! This statement will be referred to as an *accountability statement* throughout this chapter and could easily be one of the most important concepts in this book.   Before delving into the accountability statement, a review of several issues is needed.

MAJOR POINT
CEOs (generally) don't have an intimate knowledge about the job the processes, or the projects their managers are managing.

Granted, they may have come from one or possibly two of the fields or positions that their key managers oversee, but they often don't know the intimate details of the six to eight positions they may be managing. So, how can a CEO better manage the "unknown" or day-to-day details and do so with fairness to the manager? Many believe that focusing on the "responsibilities" is the answer, when in reality this is only half of the answer. The most critical and often most elusive half, is managing accountabilities.   Each job must be divided into two parts: the *results needed* and the *responsibilities* of the manager.   The responsibilities include the day to day tasks and duties, key managers perform for the CEO and the company. The *results needed*, however, must be handed down from the CEO to his or her key managers.

MAJOR POINTS
• Responsibilities are what a person does in their job.
• Accountabilities are what the boss (and the company) needs from the job.

You would think that every person who's fairly intelligent would know exactly what the boss wants, and would be working to achieve those items. Actually, most people are surprised to find their bosses list, is a different than theirs, but that their high priorities also differ greatly. Why?   Here are just a few reasons why most people are out of touch with their boss:

Chapter 6

1. Most bosses never performed the duties the subordinate is doing.
2. Most people have a problem with committing their projects and goals to paper.
3. Most people assume that the boss knows what they're doing and agree with them in terms of their efforts.
4. Most people inherit work from the person who had the job before them.
5. Most people are reviewed by their boss once a year (if they are lucky).

While this list could be expanded, you get the idea.   Next, the interesting part is you'd think the higher you go in a corporation, the more greater importance the role accountability would play in reviews of high ranking executives and his or her managers.   Not really.   The key word here would be trust. Often, presidents hire high ranking personnel to handle specific functions and then just trusts that he or she will the function correctly and in the manner the president perceives the function should be performed. Many times the individual hired is operating from a job description, devoid of any type of accountability statement.   Yes, it is loaded with responsibilities from the past, but it is frequently so out of date as to be missing any valid accountability statement.   From the top down, this problem is repeated at many levels when hiring of key managers and professional people.

The important missing part is what is needed from the job and not how it is to be performed.

MAJOR POINTS
• It is the boss' obligation to tell the subordinate what their account abilities are.
• It is the subordinate's obligation to incorporate those accountabilities into their daily functions.

One of the major reasons people get laid off, or just let go is that their accountabilities are never understood or valued at a higher level. The irony is, the departing employee person may have understood their responsibilities, yet may never have understood their accountabilities.

How many times have you heard a person say, "that is not what they hired me to do."   This is a classic example of responsibilities versus accountabilities and its lack of clarification.

MAJOR POINT
Managers don't have to know details of the jobs they are managing, but they MUST know the results they need.

In short, it is the manager's obligation to know what results are needed, and it is the employees' obligation to know how to do the job (which brings about the results that are needed). A simple division of these two words should guide you through the process. What is the manager's part, how is the subordinate's part.

You hire a person whom you assume knows how to perform his or her function. They have experience performing that function and are assumed to be qualified, but frequently they inherit, create, and manufacture duties, which take them away from what the company needs from that position.

Only a few functions remain pure to the results needed by the company. Sales is probably the purest because we can track sales to determine a person's results rather accurately. However, even sales can get muddy. Veteran sales people will often stop building sales within their territories because of burnout, excessive travel, family demands, loss of enthusiasm, wanting more money, and the list goes on. When you consider ALL other company functions, such as accounting, manufacturing, marketing, purchasing, etc., and how they affect one another, tracking results gets complicated, very quickly.

Complications, Respect and Distractions

MAJOR POINT
Activity $\neq$ Effort $\neq$ Results

In math, the sign "$\neq$" means "does not equal." Therefore, the statement "Activity $\neq$ Effort $\neq$ Results" reads "activity does not equal effort, and effort does not equal results." Enter "work ethic." We've all seen people who seem to be constantly on the move. Their motion is their signature pattern. They seem to be away from the desk, taking something to someone, traveling, or "in the shop." On the results side of the picture, they are chronically late with reports and tasks needing completion. A conclusion to be drawn is that their activity does not equate with effort. They're constantly busy but aren't putting forth much effort. Careful, the company might have a key manager who is always "busy" in the field but, as mentioned above, is late with critical reports, projects assigned, and tasks to be completed.

Chapter 6

The second part of the business equation is effort. Here's a classic example. We all have seen the sixty-to-seventy-hour manager who just kills the company with time and effort. He or she is usually the first one in and sometimes the last one out. This person's efforts are hard to ignore, as this type of work ethic is hard to condemn. Or is it? Consistent, seventy-hour work weeks rarely produce effective results as the person is generally in a mental fog. We're not talking about getting ready for a major meeting or presentation, but rather a chronic work pattern. Again, what are the person's results? Do they seem to be ahead of the game or always catching up? Do they produce results or just kill you with effort? If you are a typical manager, you know what results you are not getting from these types. Add tenure to the picture and you have a hard-working, most likely very loyal, person who has been around for years, but may not be providing the results you need.

Accountability Statement

Where do you start in preparing an accountability statement for each of your people? Here is a quick checklist:

1. Make a quick list of your people.
2. Prioritize the list with the #1 person being the one for which you need to establish the accountability parameters first. Your greatest challenge as a manager.
3. Continue through the list until it is completely prioritized for all your people. Don't stop with the first few. Complete the list.
4. Take the first #1 person and think about what you need that is not currently being done.
5. Do a random list of items, being brief and to the point. Don't worry about grammar and sentence structure. Just put down the content of what you think you need.
6. Keep the list of items on one page (or a computer document of one page).
7. Put the list away for a day.
8. The next day, prioritize the list and rewrite it with any embellishments you feel you need.
9. Have a meeting with the person and review the list. Careful, here is where the fun begins. Most likely, the person will defend their position with lists of responsibilities and think in terms of what they have been doing, not in terms of what you want them to do. However, agreement is a must between you and your subordinate
10. Repeat the process with the next highest person you prioritized.

It should be pointed out that the list created is not intended to be an indictment in terms of performance. The basic objective is to focus on those individuals who need improvement using a constructive methodology.

MAJOR POINT
The process of creating and doing accountability statements may flush out some people.

Some people may leave the company due to the process of holding them accountable. This may result in personnel losses both at higher levels within a company as well as lower level personnel. Sometime, a person performing a key job within the company will find the accountability to be compromising to their views of where the company is heading or what areas of business the company should be involved in. While this process may act as a catalyst in their leaving, holding people accountable, is not only the best method for obtaining desired results, it is best for the company as well.

Job Descriptions

"I'll know it when I see it." This is probably one of the worst things a president or manager can say. From an employee's perspective, trying to please a person who tells you this is very frustrating. Work is not a Rorschach test. Shooting at moving targets that are hit-or-miss for the employee is not the employee's problem. It is the manager's. "Tell me what you want and I'll deliver it" is what truly motivated employees need to maintain morale.

Nevertheless, there are a lot of managers who relish not having job descriptions. In addition, there are books that support that direction. Hogwash! Job descriptions are necessary--period. The **what** and **how** needs to be combined (remember the **what** is what you need a person to do and **how** is basically the responsibilities of the person in the job). The greatest fear of a manager, who doesn't want job descriptions, is that the person(s) being managed will not reach for responsibility, beyond their defined job description. Again, hogwash! Good people will always reach out and do a good job if the climate, culture, and attitude of the company are positive. They will leave when these things are not happening.

Chapter 6

Effective Job Descriptions:
Combine the Responsibilities with the Accountabilities

Creating an effective job description may sound complicated but it's not really. Just take the existing job description, staple the accountability statement to it, and you could be done for now. OK, Human Resources will want more, but do you need more? Not really, and not for now. Next, until a company sets its growth goals, this may be as much as you can do for now. At this stage of creating an effective job description, you want to pin down what you haven't been receiving from a key manager; make that manager aware of the discrepancies, and reconcile the differences.

Summary of the Steps Necessary for an Effective Job Description

Description:
1. Take a copy of the existing job description (if one exists) and read it.
2. Highlight the areas that you don't feel are necessary or that need further clarification.
3. Take the accountability section you completed earlier and reread it to make sure you agree with what you said prior to looking at the existing job description.
4. Change or edit the new accountability section if needed.
5. Call in the person and review both the existing job description and the new accountability section.
6. Allow the person to make his or her points about any differences he or she sees or wants to make.
7. Change either the original job description or your account ability section if you feel they have a valid point, but remember, the person might be doing things historically that yield little or no current value in terms of results needed for that job.
8. As stated earlier, staple the two together: the existing job description or any revisions and the accountability section, or any revisions.
9. Keep the documents in a separate file for future discussions.
10. You might return to this document when your company determines what their growth goals are for the company, and how this person fits into those goals.

MAJOR POINT
What you need from a key manager that you are not getting now, must always be defined in terms of results, not activity, not effort, but results.

Company Growth Goal Setting

It could be debated that a company should wait until they've set their company growth goals before doing a series of individual accountability statements. This is really a "Catch 22" scenario. What comes first, learning the process of accountability or setting company goals and factoring these into the individual accountability statements? The real answer here is, it just depends on the company and their commitment (or lack of commitment) to defining company goals.

In my last book, *"Grow or Die: Growth Strategies for Management"*,` the entire book focuses on targeting and managing real growth. *"Grow or Die"*, is available in print at www.amazon.com\book\growordiegrowthstrategiesformanagement. This should be considered by anyone who is a key manager, president or business owner.

Cultivating The One Page Manager

This chapter is written to encourage the President, Vice Presidents, and key business managers to cultivate the One Page manager system, as an effective means of increasing accountability, productivity and results throughout their company. While a Vice President can promote the One Page Manager methodology for his area of responsibility, the real impetus for company-wide success and results, rests with the President.

All top level executives and managers would like all of the people who work for them to be self-managed.

Exactly what is self-management? Self-management is having subordinates reporting to you, who pro-actively review their own work with you without being asked, selecting goals with which you and they both agree and completing their work on time, as they predicted. As soon as you read this (if you are the boss), I am sure you'll say, "Right, and I will win the lottery next week!"

The simple truth is, if you follow the steps outlined in this book, you CAN create a complete staff of self-managed employees. This chapter concentrates on the steps your company needs to take to cultivate self-motivated managers, with the One Page Manager system.

The State of the Union Meeting

First, why does a company need a State of the Union Meeting? In a sentence: to establish the direction for key managers in the company. Frequently, those managers are craving direction and a clear understanding of where the company is headed for the future. Rarely is this subject covered in meetings and if it is, it's generally as an after-thought. This meeting should start and end with the company direction being defined and discussed.

This meeting should include top executives and key managers only.

Each participant should incorporate the goals, within their area of responsibility, which they believe will accomplish the overall vision. The President should confirm or re-direct Goals to insure to correct path for achieving the company mission.

Chapter 7

The Announcement Letter

A letter announcing the meeting should go out at least two weeks before the meeting. It should have as an attachment, an agenda with times for each participant/presenter worked out. Careful here, meeting schedulers often under estimate the time per speaker, especially the question and answer time. As a general rule, allow at least one hour per speaker with a clear understanding that questions allowed or not will not be allowed during the presentations. If you allow questions during presentations you'll need a facilitator to monitor time and maintain schedules for all presenter(s).

The letter should include the dates, the location address (adding a map is helpful), and the dress code for the meetings and events as necessary.

Critical to the meeting is the preliminary preparation of their Goals Page illustrating their perceived goals, tasks and priorities in keeping with their department and company goals. This preliminary Goals Page must be prepared in prior to the first meeting.

Brief Departmental Reviews

The emphasis of this meeting is "the future", not the past.

Insist the each departmental presentation focus 75% of their presentation on achieving future company growth, with only 25% of their presentation dealing with historical issues or recent preparations for the future.

Easily, each presenter can occupy all of their presentation time telling you what their department has done in the last 12 to 6 months. .

Presentation of Key Managers Goals

As stated earlier, there are three types of goals: company, departmental, and individual. Only a few participants will have company goals requiring a matrix development page. Almost everyone else, should be presenting and discussing departmental goals.

The format is to present each Key Manager's Goals Page to the group with a breakdown of specifics, as necessity. Remember, the group is generally not interested in **how** a person is going to accomplish their respective goal. Only the **what**, **priority**, and the **when** of the goal. The detail or tactics are the domain of the individual and their function.

Time for Questions and Answers

This part can get tricky. The facilitator must monitor Q&A time carefully to keep meetings on schedule. Questions can be answered quickly, should be addressed at the end of the presentation. On the other hand, complicated questions, which require in-depth technical explanations, should be scheduled for discussion the following day in the group round table discussion.

Not too infrequently, this question and answer period will involve two people within the company that have squared off previously in group sessions. This is quite healthy in companies that allow for open disagreement, so topics or issues can be discussed from different points of views. However, if this is left unchecked, the debate can sometimes take up too much valuable meeting time. Again, this is where the facilitator must control the discussion with care and move the topic to the next day. The facilitator may needs more information about topics which could potentially occupying too much time in the next day's round table. If touchy, the facilitator should seek Presidential help in mediating the subject.

The facilitator should be using a flip chart to record major subjects for the next day's round table. Care should be taken to prioritize the subjects to place the most important subject first with less important items at the end. This will allow the most time for the most important subjects.

Round Table Discussion

The following day should see the group discussing subjects recorded the previous day on the flip chart, plus pertinent topics people might wish to add, time permitting. This is a very important part of the meeting, in which, participants have an opportunity to express their feelings and view points regarding the topics presented. It should be a rather "no holds bared" session, however, proper decorum, courtesy and respect must be maintained at all times. People should be allowed to voice concern about goals or their accomplishment.

The key to this part of the meeting is to remain creative in nature, with positive suggestions, and comments. While criticism is allowed, it should be limited. Telling someone something is wrong is OK, providing a creative solution to solve the issue, is also provided.

The facilitator should record all comments into a list. This list can be typed up later and distributed to all participants. Care should be taken not only to list the comments relative to the subject, but the person (wherever possible) should be entered on the sheet with the responsibility of performing each newly required tasks. Finally, a time parameter should be established (where possible).

Updates and Corrections

An important part of the process is understanding that corrections to the binder/pass-outs must be made and accepted. The President should insist corrections to the Goals Pages and that the persons having specific functional responsibility to each area agrees with those changes. Essentially, we're talking about improvements, additional items/goals, or corrections to the content of the presentation. As a check and balance system, the President should make comments on his/her copy of the pass-outs to insure all participants update their improvements.

A Meeting to Discuss and Learn about the Goals Page

There are meetings held every day in thousands of companies, after which, most of the participants will tell you was a waste of time. Given the proper explanation of the foundation and rationale of this system, this will not be one of those meetings. It is important, however, that participants understand the methodology prior to starting their first Goals Page.

Presidential Message

As stated earlier, the President should lead this meeting.   Many Presidents will let a Vice President take leadership in meetings, but in this meeting the CEO should set the tone by endorsing the methodology of the One Page Manager system.

Tips to the top man:

1.   Do not wing your part of this meeting.   Prepare for and hold yourself accountable for your presentation. Treat the attendees like they are investors.
2.   Start the meeting with your "State of the Union" message to the group.
3.   Do not be afraid to admit what you don't know.
4.   Remember, the people in the room want direction. Give it to them.
5.   Use visuals as means to communicate your message.

The point of your message as President is to give them vision and insight into where the company is heading.   Growth is essential.   How will you grow, what resources will the company need, and who will be responsible for what parts?   A new location for the plant, a new emphasis on new products or services, ISO or GS undertakings or revisited to be more meaningful, planning that is held accountable (with dates, not just subjects), an IPO in the future, are all examples for tomorrows direction.

MAJOR POINT

Hey, you da man (or da woman). Without your vision, the company is generally blind. That is your primary role.

Stress one important point. The company will have follow-up on this concept. There will be 30 to 60 day reviews of all the Goals Pages and accomplishments will be part of your annual review, but held in 30 to 60 day windows.

Accountability Versus Responsibility

Here is a quick explanation of two very important words and concepts.

MAJOR POINTS
• Responsibilities are what a person does in their jobs.
• Accountabilities are what the boss needs done.

The word accountability is very fashionable in business today. While many articles may explain or expand why it's important, the real questions is "How do you reach it with your employees and managers?" In the preceding chapter on accountability, there were two definite means of identifying a person's accountability. They were:
1.   The use of the Goals Page to identify and record the account abilities.
2.   If the items were not part of the person's job description, a method of updating the job description to include a section for accountabilities separate from their responsibilities.

In the case of the Goals Page, it's a simple methodology for a manager or supervisor to add any missing parts to an employee's Goals Page. There are two checklists in chapter six on accountability that should help the manager through the steps necessary to complete an update.

1. Sending the Message about Accountability to the Company

Without the President or other high ranking management endorsements at this meeting to the concept of accountability, the potential for results concerning accountability could be jeopardized. Undoubtedly, there are some people in every company who will only "play" at this concept if top management is not committed to it. Why? These people historically resist putting their actions in writing to avoid being accountable for anything. It must be made clear that this is no game and the company is serious about doing it.

Conversely, there are willing self-managers and self-starters who will find no difficulty in doing a Goals Page and desire the results they are trying to achieve. These will be your best performers who desire recognition for their efforts.

The marginal performers will also stand out with this system and the company should be aware of this potential   Bottom line: the group in attendance at this meeting will sense the seriousness of accountability and the emphasis placed on results.

2. Reward Accountability

Consider some means of an initial reward system for people who complete the first drafts of their Goals Page on time, and start to achieve the results as they document their Goals Page.   This will promote a positive attitude for all employees as they improve and show increased results.   Consider American Express gift certificates for a dinner for two, points for results, or some other means of recognition.. Remember, these ideas are for initial start-up of the concept and not a long term program.

Common Company Language

As a consultant, I typically pass out a simple one page set of words, which I feel are key to any company conducting, creating, or producing a business plan.   The words are: strategic, goal, objective, strategy, tactics, planning, and actions plans. I ask the individuals to write their definition for each word, right next to the one in print. The test is also administered to all key managers in the company (generally 6 to 8 people).

The results are predictable.   Rarely do any of the individual definitions match anyone else's, given some latitude for interpretation.
Why? Because each person's educational level, vocational pursuits, and educational backgrounds and perspectives (finance versus marketing etc.) are different.

MAJOR POINT
It is not important that you determine an exact definition of key words; however, it is imperative that you agree internally on company definitions for those words.

While my definitions for these words are purposely simple and concise, yours may vary. Regardless of personal differences, these key words and concepts need a consistency of meaning when being used in meetings, planning documents, and during personnel reviews.

Defining and Setting Priorities

If you are a President, Vice President, or a key manager who does not believe in setting priorities, this book may have little value to you. I once worked for a President who took pride in using the expression, "I'll know it when I see it." He simply did not believe in setting priorities for the people who worked for him. His fear was that if they set a priority, something else would not get done. Consequently, many hours of frustration resulted within his staff and key managers. Many meetings took place with his silent expressions much more of an impact than any words he used. A President is a working partner with his subordinates, not a monarch ruling the land.

MAJOR POINT
There is sometimes a fine line between service and servants and the feelings passed on to your people.

The word used in the title of this chapter was deliberately picked. Cultivating self-management is based on honest dialogue and a genuine need for input for each person. You can grow confident managers and subordinates if you help them set their priorities.

The process is rather simple: You let them first tell you what they feel the priorities are, and then add yours. If they consistently avoid or select poor priorities, you may either have a weak manager or the wrong manager for the job.

Real producers, not only perform well in their jobs, but they can generally predict their results in advance.

Selecting Meaningful Goals

Most bosses can look at the Goals Page and tell, almost immediately, if the individual has the horsepower to do the job. The indicators are generally self-evident. How long is the list? Does it cover subjects that have been discussed before (is the person listening to you or does the person have their own agenda)? Does the individual take risks? Are they pro-active?

Chapter 7

MAJOR POINT
Pro-active means to anticipate and take the next step without being told.

While pro-activity can be cultivated, I don't think it can be taught. There's an instinct relative to what that next step is and the anticipation of where they're going. People who have it are destined to reach higher levels. People who don't have it, are not. Add the ability to take risks to the equation and you have the right person.

A great indicator is the original list of goals submitted. That list will tell you a lot.

Most people who are selected to attend this meeting realize they are being scrutinized in terms of the goals submitted. Prior to this meeting they might have submitted weak or poor goals as an attempt to "beat the system." After the meeting, the list of goals and the bar will be much higher. They know what's at stake and that they're being held accountable for what they've chosen, in addition to whatever the boss will add to the list to keep the process honest (the selection of meaningful goals).

Presenting The One Page Manager System

All chapters in The One Page Manager should be passed out and digested prior to this meeting. Critical to the meeting is the understanding of the One Page/Goals Page concept. Next, an understanding of the matrix as a tool followed by the project list concept. Both are essential to the success of the total One Page Manager system and its deployment.

This part of the meeting can involve questions and answers concerning the concepts, the horizontal nature of planning (laying out the sheets developed and seeing them all at once), and finally understanding multi-tasking is essential in today's business world. Doing one thing at a time and until complete is a luxury not a practical reality.

A consultant or delegated moderator/facilitator is very important. Someone must know the components of the system to present them and answer questions. The chapters on Accountability and Common Company Language need to be presented and discussed in-depth.

First Scheduled Session with the "One Page/Goals Page"

At this point in time, each person who created their Goals Page has neither received their bosses priorities or his or her new additions to the list. The State of the Union Meeting is giving the individuals side of the picture as they see it. After the meeting, each manager will have an opportunity to review the meeting reports and any dialogue concerning the subject by the group members, or changes the manager feels is appropriate. Remember, it is a report as it contains both departmental information and the Goals Page.

The boss should mark-up a copy of the report and return it with these potential changes:
1. Any additional comments or items to add
2. The priorities that the boss determines for that person's goals from the original
3. Any additional comments that would prepare the individual for the first meeting

The first meeting could take place several days after returning the original copy back to the person, and given a mutual time for the meeting.

The important part to remember is if a manager adds several items to an employee's list, it might take a few days for that employee to prepare comments about the subject. It's probably a given the manager will have added items to the list, but the manager should allow the employee the opportunity to ask questions about why the subjects are being added, especially if the item is sensitive between the two.

MAJOR POINT
It's imperative the employee leaves the meeting agreeing to the new items, understanding the difference between their priorities, and understanding the accountabilities listed.

The point of the meeting is to establish a clear understanding what's expected of the employee from the manager's perspective and the employee. The expectations include the completion of the goals, the time of completion for each item, and the importance of those items stated in a numerical order: their priority.

Chapter 7

Scheduled Meetings for Follow-Up

It is just too easy to have the first meeting and then procrastinate for future meetings. All kinds of reasons enter in to "why" the next meeting could not be held for months, such as, vacations, trade show attendance, travel to customer locations, etc. The manager must pencil in dates and stick to them, changing the dates only if REALLY necessary.

Beware of the excuse. The subordinate is being held accountable for their actions and more importantly, results. There's a human tendency to delay bad news, or fail to report bad news, especially if they've not gotten around to doing what they said they would. Don't let up on results that are needed. Results don't just happen. Results entail a lot of work.

Business Talk:
Common Business Language

What if we compare a company to an orchestra? Each department is a section of the orchestra and needs to learn its own part. When the conductor picks up the baton, all sections work together into a sound that blends. The problem starts when musicians don't read the same notes with the same meaning. An orchestra is a very cohesive group which plays within a very exact set of musical parameters. If one group does "its own thing," the sound is wrong and both the audience and conductor instantly hears it.

In order for any company to reach accord and work together, they must first talk the same language.

MAJOR POINTS

Business people need to talk the same talk. They must be playing off their same sheet of music: the Goals Page. The company does not have a single sheet of music, but should be operating from a complete musical score: the business plan.

In any planning meeting 10 key words and phrases, inevitably come up. Each person using these words will probably have a different meaning. So the logic prevails that if people in business use these words, the words should have the same approximate meaning regardless of who uses the words.

Next, regardless of their educational and experience differences, the people involved should be communicating on common ground. No college, junior college, degrees, state university, advanced degree(s), should make a difference when communicating these important concepts and ideas that the words represent.

MAJOR POINT

People in the same company need to use key words and concepts in the same way if the company is to be successful

It is not important that you've learned, or been taught different definitions to key words and concepts., the important issue, is that you use the words, in the same way the company you are working for, defines them. I would recommend you challenge these definitions and change them if they don't fit your culture. Next, add to the list if you feel there are words used

Chapter 8

regularly in your meetings. But, don't use the words as you see fit or allow people who are controlling the destiny of your company to use them without regard to their importance, and most of all, mutual understanding.

Returning to the point of challenging these definitions:

It is OK to change the definition of the words defined if, and this is a big if, all the people involved in planning agree to the new definition. There is not much you can do if the owner, CEO, or president disagrees with the definition of a word but go along with his or her definition. The important part, again, is that all who are involved with planning in the company change to the new definition.

The following words have been deliberately made simple. The problem with going to a Webster's Dictionary is that the words defined, are generalized and are not specific for the business world and the common use of these words. If you disagree or challenge their definition, this chapter was completely worth the time taken to read it and digest it.

10 Key Words and Concepts and their Defined Meanings:

1. Strategic

Never has a word been more frequently used in business, yet so poorly defined. Most dictionaries define strategic as "necessary to or important in the initiation, conduct, or completion of a strategic plan; of great importance within an integrated whole or to a planned effect."

Here we see a good example of the dictionary's general definition of the word. Practically speaking, if the word is used alone, it means **important.** Frequently, it is use with another word (strategic plan, strategic maneuver etc.). Therefore, consider it a half of two words. If it is used as two words, the definition of important still applies. When used in a planning sense, it is implied to be longer in time duration then just a short range concept.

As suggested earlier, most people would have a difficult time defining the word. Just make sure you all agree with its definition.

2. Goal

Another heavily used word that is often used interchangeably with the word "objective" and sometimes to a lesser degree "strategy" is substituted for the word goal. The dictionary defines goal as "the terminal point of a race; the end toward which effort is directed."

A "goal" like the word "strategic" implies a longer duration than an "objective" and should not be used interchangeably with the word "strategy". I would define the word "goal" to be **a long range effort that has a terminal point that is difficult to measure and that is generally a wish or direction for the company.** Having said that, I would say that "goals" are a starting point, for all company efforts. They are very valuable as they start the planning process.

Here is a very easy definition that I use often when defining the word in a meeting: it is the **result you wish to accomplish.**

3. Strategic Goal

Since strategic and goal, have been defined, we can proceed to put these two word together as follows: a strategic goal is **an important result that a company desires to accomplish.** Once defined and selected, the entire resource of the company should be directed toward the concept. A company should choose a strategic goal with a great deal of deliberation, study, and agreement from the key managers of the company due to the importance of the selection.

I believe a company should keep to a minimum the number of strategic goals that should be considered. If too many goals are considered, it will dilute the resources of the company. I have listed eight in my book entitled, "Grow or Die: Growth Strategies for Management." Each has been carefully chosen to make sure that the accomplishment of that goal would result in an increased in business or a necessary building block for the future of the company.

Here are the eight goals listed in "Grow or Die: Growth Strategies for Management."
1. Target SKU (standard catalogue units) growth
2. Sell more products to your existing customers
3. Hang on to existing market share
4. Target new customers with existing products
5. Attack competition (generally one major player)
6. Target new markets with existing products
7. Design new products internally
8. Buy new products for resale

Chapter 8

4. Objective

Objective, and another key word strategy, are both used to describe concepts. Both are used with equal in magnitude.
An objective is "**what**" you do that leads to results defined by a goal.   It must meet three criteria:

   1.   **It must be measurable**
   2.   **It must be over a time parameter.**
   3.   **It must be realistic.**

An objective is not a goal.   These two words: goals and objectives are not interchangeable. The objective is derivative of a goal and not the other way around.

An objective is the expansion of a goal as it further defines the goal from a desired result into an entity that is then measured, put over time, and finally must meet the test of realism.   An example is given to the reader in Chapter Three- Matrixes.

5. Strategy

A strategy is "**how**" you will do something.   The Marketing Strategy encompassed two basic elements:

   1.   **The market target (who is the strategy aimed at)**
   2.   **The marketing mix (where the how's come from):**
      a.   **Product**
      b.   **Price**
      c.   **Place / Channels of distribution**
      d.   **Promotion**
      e.   **People (the Sales Force)**

While the above definition has its major application in the marketing of products or services, each department of a company (operations, manufacturing, accounting, etc.) will have its own set of elements or its own functional mix.   To attempt to define each set of elements for each department is beyond the scope of this book.   But, the recognition of the differences must be pointed out.

The reader is asked to also recall the first chapter in this book and the list of results that most companies desire as well. Each department or function will have its own set of strategies to consider, but these must be directed to the strategic goals that the company has defined or identified.   Strategic goals established by the company and its leadership come first and have the highest priority.

6. Tactics

A tactic is the "who", "when", and possibly the "where" of the strategy. It is the details of the strategy broken-down by the specific of the actions to be performed. Highly related to the tactics derived from the strategy is an action plan or schedule.

Therefore, **the action plan is the document that show the tactics in a graphic (columnar format) of the "when", "how", "who", and "where" of the strategy.** Each objective should have its own set of strategy or strategies and related tactics.

7. Business Plan

A group of actions organized by departments and should be focused toward the accomplishment of the strategic goals chosen by the company. It's a written document authored by the department heads of the company responsible for the functions found within the document. Every department head should take full responsibility for its own written and managed section. In many respects it is the bible of the company and should be treated with a great deal of serious effort.

8. Marketing Plan

A written document which outlines, for the company or individual departments, the intended efforts for accomplishing strategic goals of the company. It should involve the following sections and implied activities: Facts of the company, Situation Analysis / Strengths & Weakness, Objectives, Strategies, Tactics / Action Plan, Sales Forecast, and Budget.

9. Departmental Plans

A departmental plan is a section of the business plan generally divided by the department or functions found within the company. The departmental plan should inform the company of what, how, and when the major activities of that department are to be performed. Key to the success of that company is that the department plans must reflect the growth portions those activities first and support the strategic goals of the company with the highest priority.

Chapter 8

10. Situation Analysis / Strengths & Weaknesses

A situation analysis is an in-depth study on products, pricing, channels of distribution, programs, promotions and policies. This is a very important concept. "We know what are our strengths and weaknesses are, so why do an analysis?" Easy answer. Every department will probably give you either a different answer or one that will be worded and phased differently. Again, all departments must be playing from the same score of music or else the discord will be heard and the result of this difference will be a problematic to the company. If Manufacturing thinks that a product improvement is a significant weakness, but Marketing doesn't regard this as significant, you have a problem.

> ## MAJOR POINT
> • A situation analysis is done so that everyone that is key to the company's   success is aware of the same strengths and weakness.
> • A plan is created for the benefit of everyone, not for the sake of an individual department. Everyone must read and agree!

Companies constantly hear complaints that there is not enough time to write a plan.

This cannot be tolerated by upper management. You have to make the time, if you're going to increase sales and grow the company. There's a definite correlation between planning and success. Careful, I did not say the plan, but planning. If you're updating the plan, you're planning. If you do the plan once a year, you are not planning!

> ## MAJOR POINT
> Planning is a process, not a product (the plan).

"Failing to prepare is preparing to fail."
Benjamin Franklin

Unfortunately, most businesses, owners, managers and employees focus so much of their energies handling daily demands, that they have little time or mental endurance left for planning or managing their future success.

The systems provided by The One Page Manager, eliminates wasted time, effort and misdirected goals. The systems improve planning, communications and efficiency to yield real results, for those who use them.

Donald M. Urbaniec
Professional Biography

Don Urbaniec is President of DMU & Associates, a business consulting firm specializing in developing client growth through a systems approach published in Grow or Die: Growth Strategies for Management. Don has over 35 years of professional experience spanning functions, which include corporate planning, sales, marketing and communications.

He has held positions as Corporate and Sales Planning Manager, Director of Marketing, Manager of Marketing Communications, and as a full partner in an advertising agency. Don's formal work background includes working for a multi-billion dollar corporation, a 100 million dollar corporation and additional multi-million dollar companies.

Don's academic credentials include a Bachelors in Marketing and a Masters in Business Administration from California State University at Long Beach. In addition, he designed, developed and formerly taught a course on new product development entitled, New Product Development Procedures 2000.

DMU & Associates
21W041 Monticello
Lombard, IL 60148

E-mail: urbaniec@comcast.net

Grow or Die: Growth Strategies for Management, is available in print form at www.amazon.com. The One Page Manager, is available in either print or Kindle form at www.amazon.com.

www.ingramcontent.com/pod-product-compliance
Lightning Source LLC
Chambersburg PA
CBHW081844170526
45167CB00007B/2897